Up North

poems by

Neal Zirn

Finishing Line Press
Georgetown, Kentucky

Up North

ACKNOWLEDGMENTS

These poems were first published in the following journals:

After the Divorce—*Mudfish*
Everything Passes—*Mudfish*
Country Boy—*Blueline*
Up North—*Blueline*
She's Probably Still There—*The Big Windows Review*—Nominated for Best of
the Net 2023
New to Single Parenting—*Paterson Literary Review*/Honorable Mention
Allen Ginsberg Poetry Contest
Mistaken Identity—*Poetica*
Hunting Season—*Nerve Cowboy*

Publisher: Leah Huete de Maines
Editor: Christen Kincaid
Cover Art: Neal Zirn
Author Photo: Neal Zirn
Cover Design: Elizabeth Maines McCleavy

Order online: www.finishinglinepress.com
also available on amazon.com

Author inquiries and mail orders:
Finishing Line Press
PO Box 1626
Georgetown, Kentucky 40324
USA

Table of Contents

Dedicated to my children:
Ramona, Deirdre, and Nicholas

Practicing Tai Chi Alongside the Raquette River

Nothing moves but the turning of the waist,
and the blue heron that skims the water,
and the centuries past.

Mistaken Identity

I see them all the time now,
in their old-country clothes,
the men in black hats and beards,
the women with their heads covered,
riding alongside the road in their horse-drawn
wagons. For a long time now, people up here
thought the Chabad Rabbi, in his old country
clothes, black hat, and beard, walking alongside
the road with his wife, who covered her head,
was one of them. Amish.

One Cat

I was driving in farm country,
the fields already turned over
for the winter, the air a mix
of wood stoves and what was
to follow, when my vision
picked up an orange and white
blur, to my left, as it continued
to gain ground at what was
an alarming speed, until it
slammed into the front-end
of my vehicle, then remained
quite still as if it were seated
in church, on the centerline
of the road, its hind legs crushed
and useless as a rusted-out plow,
the last of its many lives spreading
surreptitiously, like a morning fog,
seeping into the smooth, black asphalt.

April Upstate,

a dog of a time,
tractor stuck out in a field,
one wheel flat, with nothing
to turn over but a few lace
pillows, this barn swallow
morning whistling its way
in through a window left
open, coffee on the stove,
cats calling as if they'd never
been fed, legs stiff, back stiffer,
the house silent like an early
motion picture, the last of your
will, strong, stoic, and ready
for the planting, this absence
that is mine bringing in its fold,
a fallow tract rolling west
and the end of another season.

Sunday

They sit in the living room
of a red, beat-up house,
the trim peeling, the front
steps sloping down on one
side, two elderly women
inside a dark space, staring
out at me as I walk by on
the west side of Miner Street.

It's Sunday, the day before
Memorial Day, in this small
town in upstate New York,
and there is nothing like
old houses, old women,
and dead soldiers, to remind
me that the hills cast a shadow,
and that every front has a back,
as, stepping like a man walking
on a sea of lost causes, I cross
on over to the east, and sunny
side, of Miner Street.

Wednesday

He doesn't look that old,
maybe 35 or 40, stuck
in a wheelchair with an
oxygen tank strapped to
the back and plastic lines
running up to his nose.
He's wearing gray shorts,
a baseball cap, and his legs
are thin, like the strings on my
Martin guitar. His face is covered
with beard, and an overweight
woman is feeding him ice cream.

I pass him as I go by
the refreshment stand,
on my way to the post office,
thinking, *there by the grace*, etc.
Part of me wants to ask, *why*,
and part of me doesn't want
to give it another thought.
It's a cloudless, blue day,
a day with couples sitting
side by side on benches
in the park, and children
splashing, as if they had
flippers, by the fountain.
If it wasn't for the man,
bound to his wheelchair
like a tranquilized Buddha,
the illusion that this day
is lovely, and without fault,
would be perfect.

Like our God.

The Adirondacks

There are mountains to climb in the Adirondacks,
and roads lined with pine trees that provide a shield
to ward off the winter winds.

Driving through, I always had the feeling
that I was somewhere far away from my troubles,
that I could park by the side of the road,
climb a trail that led up a mountain,
and disappear into the mist as if I never existed,
as if my life were something I had imagined to be real.

It was a strange sensation, the remoteness of where I was,
taking me over and into recesses that were new,
and in some ways foreboding. Dreams of lost horizons
would flood my mind, and sometimes I wondered
if I would ever find my way home,

or see myself in the lost circle of time

Being From the City,

I cannot name many of the trees
in the forest nor the flowers in the field.

Perhaps, because of this lack of knowledge,
I see them as they are, plain and pristine,
as myriad shapes and colors, living their lives
within a unique silence.

The world of Nature has its own reality,
its mysteries, when revealed, are more profound
than any intellectual realizations.

When the wind blows through the pines,
there are secrets in its voice.

When a crow cries at midnight,
all is not the same.

Mist Above the Mountains

There is a fine mist above the mountains
as if atomized by an unknown being.
It breathes on its own, deep, and moist,
ingoing and outgoing. It breathes as the Earth
breathes as it rotates upon its axis.

I plan to be there with the coming of the spring,
hiking high above the timberline in sturdy boots
and denim jacket, taking in the view while with
each step I continue to ascend higher,

as I adjust my backpack accordingly,
carrying my share of worldly happiness
and sorrow, assigned to us as if by an ephemeral
court that is well beyond the process of appeal.

The Road Is a Song

The road is a song, winding its way
through the Adirondacks, unhurried
and free, courting the wind as if it were
a long-lost lover.

There are pine trees that overhang
both sides of my path through the mountains,
lakes, and rivers; the water covered
with dancing sunlight like jewels
in suspended animation.

It is a meditation of sorts,
far from town and city,
the rush and hum of business
a past life in the web of time.

I stop to rest and leave my car
to gaze at a cloud that appears
like a smile in the mist.

There are deer in the woods,
there are secrets in the sky,
waiting behind the day,
just out of reach.

When the Winter Winds Blew Furiously

Divorced, I felt like hiding in the back alleys
of Market Street. There wasn't much to do
for a middle-aged man who grew up
on the mean streets of the Bronx,
and wasn't aware of the customs that influenced
small town life.

Being direct was a *faux pas*, and getting things done
quickly was, well, simply out of the question.

I was used to hitting my horn if a driver didn't
get on it as soon as the light turned green.
But in St. Lawrence County, New York,
such an action was considered as rude as not shoveling
your sidewalk after a heavy snowstorm.

And trying to find a woman to date was as difficult
as locating the Lost Ark of the Covenant.

Not impossible, but something I would ponder
when the winter winds blew furiously,
and the Canadian geese made their way south.

Up North

Watch out for the deer
and the Amish buggies,
sometimes only a lantern
hanging off the back, at night,
like a radioactively enhanced
firefly, warning you of its presence
as it rolls down the road,

if you're driving up here
in the North Country, close
to Canada, where they have
a saying, "Keep your stick
on the ice," which I like to believe
refers only to men,

and the hunting season seems as if
it runs smack-dab into the fishing
season, or vice versa,

and where there is a woman I know,
living near to the borderline, whose hands
bear witness to her working the earth,
and whose kitchen is always bustling,
baking, and boiling,

and who, by now, has long since stopped
listening for the purr of my engine,
and the sound of her door closing softly
behind me.

Hunting Season

Sonofabitch, it must be hunting season again.
The men are growing their beards, and the woman
are busy canning, or cooking, or hiding from their
husbands. The rabbits, turkeys, and, most of all,
the deer, are running for their lives; across fields,
into holes, or the next county when the season
there is over. The reason for the season is called
the thinning of the herd. If the hunters didn't do it,
the winter, and the lack of food, would bring an early
death. Darwinian, so they say. Like it's never going
to happen to them; *the thinning* that is.

Winter in the North Country

I didn't snowshoe, ski, or snowmobile,
so, winter in the North Country was akin
to doing time without knowing the crime.
It was cabin fever squared. The skies
were mostly gray and foreboding.
Ice formed on the sidewalks causing
slipping and sliding at the oddest moments.
It was like Hell frozen over without the pitchforks.

I would hibernate in my room after work,
the wind rattling the windowpanes,
the trees creaking as if they were old men
assigned to assisted living, the TV babbling on
until I fell asleep.

Spring was something just out of reach,
like the ring on a carousel or the woman
you knew would never go out with you,
even if you had just hit the lottery
and had a poem published in the New Yorker.

As the season dragged on, I tried to be positive,
counted my blessings, and dreamed of flying
through the air like some great, plumed bird,
leaving what was, behind, reflecting the light
on broad, silver wings.

Elephant Eyes

The North Country has its backroads,
its farms, cows, and corn with elephant eyes
staring at the rising sun.

There is a woman who lives in a house
by the side of the road who braids her brown
hair, and reminds me of a girl I knew in grammar
school when the moon was new and the earth
contained the promise of better things to come.

I know this woman, although we haven't met yet,
and often observe her tending to her garden,
watering her plants, weeding, as necessary.

I can see her, even if she is far away,
when sitting in my room at night,
the stars scattered like so many memories
seeded in the dark.

Perhaps there are strings of light connecting
the two of us in ways I cannot understand,
unknown and hidden in the fields that are
waiting to be turned over.

Talking North Country

It's hunting and hockey, or figure skating
if that's your jam.

The winters tend to be pessimistic gray,
and sit heavy on the chest like pasta carbonara.
There's wood smoke in the air from stoves
and fireplaces, giving the surroundings a homespun,
peaceful feeling that offsets the grim reality
of the season.

Summers can be hot and humid with cloudless,
azure skies that seem to open up to the light.
Riding the backroads, the farms stretch out
across the fields, rows of feed corn planted
in military fashion.

Lives are lived in a series of peculiar small towns,
many of which peaked a long time ago,
and now shuffle about with hands in pockets,
head bent, and a blank stare that never seems to go away.

Most of the younger folks leave for better opportunities:
economically, socially, and culturally. Left behind are the aged,
like old vessels washed ashore on a beach of impending uncertainty.

If there is a saving grace, it is the remoteness of the area
that affords the inhabitants a slowness of pace and harkens
back to a more simple era when Time trod the day
in slippered feet and stopped to grace His children from afar.

Impatience

When I lived in the North Country,
I liked to ride the back roads
and take in the landscape; farms, hills,
the occasional deer or two.

Sometimes a farmer blocked my way
herding his cows across the road, rapping them
on their backsides with a stick to keep them moving.

These happenings usually brought out a certain type
of *annoyance* in me based on the fact that I had to wait
while the farmer and his cows did their thing;
like who were they to hold up my journey,
and didn't they know I had places to go and people
to see?

And that for all those years, I was not in touch
with the general flow of how things are,
involved mostly with myself, living in a way
I actually thought made sense.

Country Roads

We liked to walk the long country roads,
pass by the fields fresh with fertilizer,
watch the birds blend with the skyways,
and listen to the cayotes far off in the distance.

There was always a feeling of getting away
from it all; death and taxes, the frenzy of going
nowhere.

The illusion was that we could live in that space,
find a home where we could rest, and have the wind
at our backs, gently guiding us towards our destination.

And if there were blues on the horizon,
we didn't hear them.

And if there were chickens coming home to roost,
we didn't see them.

All we were aware of was putting one foot in front
of the other, breathing together, and the edge
of existence, which surrounded us like a forest
does the trees.

Country Boy

She said, "I can't understand it.
I never met anyone like you.
I mean, who doesn't like nature?"

And that's when I thought about
my living in the country, and how I
much preferred the police sirens
that woke me up in the Bronx
to the *damn them to hell* coyotes
that did the same thing, but kept on
at it and never stopped howling.
And how the exhaust fumes from
the city buses smelled bad, but the crap
they spread, to make things grow
on the farm next door, smelled worse.
And how my eyes puffed-up, and my nose
ran during allergy season here, like it was
racing at the Olympics, which is something
that never happened when I lived downstate.

And so, I continued to ruminate like a man
caught on a turntable. Then, with all this pecking
at my mind, I bent down and looked with care
into the face of the woman I call the Belle
of Northern New York, the one with the gap
between her two front teeth, and the sweet blue
eyes I once said were hazel, and, after all this
due consideration, answered, "Honey, I don't!"

North Country

Driving through the North Country,
there's plenty of roadkill to go around,
crows on the highway dining out,
and shacks with four-wheelers and snowmobiles
taking up space on what attempts to pass
as a front lawn.

The wind likes to come down the St. Lawrence
River Valley, at times, looking for you as if
you're one of the three little pigs about to have
his house blown down, and if the snow, ice
and lack of jobs and sunshine doesn't get you
down, there's always *the nothing to do blues*
forever playing in the background.

The trick to surviving involves putting on
your snowshoes, trudging inside yourself,
leaving behind a silent set of footprints,
and finding that place where what you
are seeing is seeing itself,

like you've been there before, but don't know,
for the life of you, when.

After the Divorce

The kids were raised in that small town
in Upstate New York, the one with two
college campuses, an old movie theatre
that looked like the fifties, and little crime
(not like where I came from) to speak of.

After the divorce, the streets seemed tired,
the ladies plain, the cops like Mayberry,
with nothing to do really being nothing
to do. I felt like a man who'd been shanghaied
on an island of ennui in the middle of a sea
of misplaced opportunity.

Everything was trivial, and love was a woman
in an alley behind the pizza place, ready to take
you out just because you happened to wander by.

Better times were hidden in a trunk in the attic
behind a picture of my patron, the Wandering
Saint of Long-Lost Causes.

Only the sound of the wind, tearing through
the pines as if it had no direction, kept me alive.

Single Life Blues

Some days it seemed like there was nothing
to do but twiddle your thumbs and stare
at your shoes. Small town life repeated
itself like the same old song sung in an echo
chamber.

When it appeared that I was at the end
of a long and twisted rope, I'd drop in
for happy hour at the local watering hole.
Back then, I'd still indulge in the occasional
beer, or two, or more, and would engage in
conversation about almost nothing at all.
I usually knew some of the patrons at the bar,
mostly professionals, who fit the big fish
in the small pond scenario.

If there was any action to be had,
I sure as shit in a windstorm couldn't
find it. My room and its four walls had more
going for it than half the population, and most
of the time it was better for me to stay home
and enjoy my own company.

I guess you could call it the single life blues
in the mindless inferno without end. Only
the gossamer-thin women, dressed like mannequins
in their Sunday best, knew how I felt.

Mostly Gray

It's mostly gray in the winter, cool gray,
crawling up your legs like it was looking
for some warmth to curl up with, nowhere
to go but up

And here you are, taking the sting out of
a dreary day, the farmland barren, snow
covered with a layer of titanium white,
the North Country slow to anger and slow
to wake up, the Canadian geese gone south
for the duration, like a gang of thieves looking
to make their final move.

And, for now, I too plan to sneak away, one last
time, after seeing you, shovel in hand clearing
your deck, knit hat with the earflaps down,
strawberry hair, gapped teeth smiling, waving
goodbye with a red mitten hand, as I head down
the freshly plowed driveway, with a firm grip
on the steering wheel, and a foot on the accelerator
that won't let up.

She's Probably Still There,

living close to the land
and the borderline, riding
her tractor, and knowing
the seasons as well as she
knows the cry of the barn
swallow and the tracks of coyotes.

She's probably still there,
fussing around her kitchen,
canning and baking pies
for the hospital fund,
her hair in ringlets,
wearing the apron that I know really
well, the one with a pattern of blue jays
and robins.

And perhaps she is so busy that I'm not
only out of sight and out of mind,
but gone completely, like the first frost
that leaves when the sun rises, and sneaks
away with the coming of the day.

North Country Women

It always seemed like the North Country
women were out to get you, grab you
by the shorthairs and give you a haircut.

Maybe it was the remoteness of the area
that bred females who procured the man
they wanted, and asked questions later.

Once they had you, it was domestication
city. The rural life came with chores to do:
fences to mend, seeds to be planted, and later,
crops to be harvested, general repair work
to be done, as necessary.

And if you happened to be the type of guy
that liked to lay about and take it easy,
well, there were consequences like the sting
of the verbal cattle prod, or the couch turning
into your new sleeping quarters.

But these women did have a distinct upside.
They knew what they wanted and weren't afraid
to reach for it.

And in a way, you were lucky to be with one of them.
They honed your rough edges, cut to the chase,
and had you forgetting who you were before you met them.

New to Single Parenting,

there was the time I took my twelve-year-old daughter,
Deirdre, to see *Goodfellas* thinking, hey, we're part
Italian, and wasn't Great Uncle Tony a made man
out in Vegas, and therefore, wasn't I just introducing her
to our heritage, right?

Or when I was with my son Nick, also about twelve
years old when this little scene took place in the big
mall in Syracuse; Nick picking up a Dr. Dre CD,
and three black gangbangers questioning me about
what I was doing, like didn't I, a white boy, know
how f-ing bad this music was?

My ex-wife, unaware of my parenting skills which,
if she knew about them, might have caused her to try
and hang my joint custody out on the line to dry.

And Nick and Deirdre, all grown up now, straighter
and saner than I ever was, despite my best efforts
to make it seem like what they thought of as *childhood*,
never really happened.

Everything Passes

Thirty years in the North Country,
practicing chiropractic, divorced,
kids on their own.

I'm here now, living in Denver,
where the mountains are high
and the marijuana is legal.

I've heard it said many times,
by people who were older than me,
that you wake up one day and wonder
where your time went, down a rabbit
hole, water under the bridge.

The small town I lived in, in retrospect,
not seeming so bad, insulated from a lot
of what goes on in this world, looking like
it did when I moved there years past,
imagining my two girls still figure skating,
my son playing hockey, patients calling me
Doc when they see me away from the office,

my sentimental memories, like smoke
from an ancient fire, following me along
the trail on the way out West.

By the Raquette

The Raquette River runs by Ives Park
where I practiced tai chi, each posture
containing a secret waiting to be discovered,
with the lineage behind me, observing
my every move.

If I listened hard enough, I could hear
the stillness, the blue heron as it glided
across the water. There was mystery
in the pines, and a depth to the sky,
that encouraged me to continue on.

When I finished the form, and bowed
to the Tao, which is beyond description,
I felt as if I could walk through walls,
or into the woods and disappear,
all the while wondering, who in this world
would know where I had gone, or take
the time to find out.

My Last Look Back at St. Lawrence County

I was certain I saw you
behind the barn near the stand
of pines, on a day when summer
turned its face away from the sun,
and autumn, on pointed toes,
let itself in, along with the early evening
star.

But it must have only been the thought
of you, reflected, and the restless nights
that kept me awake, the dreams of a clear
space on a blank, white page, and the way
we left it, cool, calm, and indifferent,
the moon on fire, screaming like sin
that hasn't seen salvation, down with
the forlorn, languishing, and lonely,
turning like a wheel in prayer, all around
Market Street.

To My Friends Back East

I can see from my balcony that it's another sunny day,
hot and dry. The skies are clear, and there, over there
to the southwest, is Pikes Peak, high and mighty, a triangle
jutting up from the earth and pointing out that Heaven is as near
as we want it to be.

I've been here two and a half months, and things are moving along.
People in my apartment elevator are kind and wish me a good day.
I'll be working in a few weeks for a program that supplies heating
assistance for those in need during the cold weather. Up to now,
it has always been so beautiful that I'm thinking, that, for variety,
it would be OK for it to, once in a while, rain all day so that,
if you're not feeling cheery at the time, here would be an opportunity
to express yourself.

I'm fine with the altitude, but the lack of moisture is doing something
to my hair, causing it to grow faster, curl, and making it look like I have
silver wings coming out of the side of my head. But then, I couldn't fool
any of you, knowing that I've never been a here-on-earth angel, or
    anything
close.

I miss most of you, some more than others, and still think of my old
    sweetie,
and what it would be like to show up one day and have that sort of
    romantic
reunion that rips your heart to pieces and says, "There, see, this is who
    you
really are, this is what you've been waiting for all your life." But the
    majority
of us have surmised, quite correctly, that things like this usually never
    happen.

Well then, hello to you and those you hold dear, from Denver. God Bless,
and please add another log to the home fires, for me. And keep them
    burning,

as best you can, in these, the times that seem as if there is no time left, even for taking some of it off.

Neal Zirn was born and raised in the Bronx. He is a retired chiropractor. His work has appeared in a host of journals including *Blueline, Mudfish, Concho River Review, The Dalhousie Review, California Quarterly, Barbaric Yawp, The Big Windows Review, The Dalhousie Review, The Main Street Rag, The Paterson Literary Review, Coal City Review, New York Quarterly* and *North Dakota Quarterly.* He has placed seven times in the Allen Ginsberg Poetry contest and been nominated for a Pushcart Prize and a Best of the Net 2023 award. His chapbook, *Manhattan Cream*, was published by MuscleHead Press.

Neal Zirn has exhibited as a painter, printmaker, and illustrator. He received a Liquitex Excellence in Art, Student Grant and placed first, and second in WCNY Art Invitationals. His drawings have appeared in *Nerve Cowboy*, and he has done illustrated chapbook covers for poets Steve Henn and William Michaelian, and poet/ flash fiction author Francine Witte.

www.ingramcontent.com/pod-product-compliance
Lightning Source LLC
Chambersburg PA
CBHW022047080426
42734CB00009B/1270